World Almanac® Library

Please visit our Web site at: www.garethstevens.com
For a free color catalog describing World Almanac® Library's
list of high-quality books and multimedia programs,
call 1-800-848-2928 (USA) or 1-800-387-3178 (Canada).
World Almanac® Library's fax: (414) 332-3567.

Library of Congress Cataloging-in-Publication Data available upon request from publisher.
Fax (414) 336-0157 for the attention of the Publishing Records Department.

ISBN-13: 978-0-8368-7925-4 (lib. bdg.)
ISBN-13: 978-0-8368-7932-2 (softcover)

This North American edition first published in 2007 by
World Almanac® Library
A Member of the WRC Media Family of Companies
330 West Olive Street, Suite 100
Milwaukee, Wisconsin 53212 USA

"The Legends of King Arthur" adapted by Seymour Reit, illustrated by Ernie Colón from "The Sword and the Stone," "The Deadly Gift," and "The Masked Defender," classic Arthurian legends. Copyright © 1992 by Bank Street College of Education. Created in collaboration with *Boys' Life* magazine. First published in *Boys' Life* magazine, August 1992, by the Boy Scouts of America. Reprinted by permission of Bank Street College of Education and *Boys' Life* magazine.

"Don Quixote" adapted by Seymour Reit, illustrated by Ernie Colón from *Don Quixote* by Miguel de Cervantes Saavedra. Copyright © 1990 by Bank Street College of Education. Created in collaboration with *Boys' Life* magazine. First published in *Boys' Life* magazine, June 1990, by the Boy Scouts of America. Reprinted by permission of Bank Street College of Education and *Boys' Life* magazine.

"The Adventures of Sherlock Holmes: The Mystery of the Blue Diamond" adapted by Seymour Reit, art by Ernie Colón from "The Adventure of the Blue Carbuncle" by Arthur Conan Doyle. Copyright © 1993 by Bank Street College of Education. Created in collaboration with *Boys' Life* magazine. First published in *Boys' Life* magazine, April 1993, by the Boy Scouts of America. Reprinted by permission of Bank Street College of Education and *Boys' Life* magazine.

This U.S. edition copyright © 2007 by World Almanac® Library.

World Almanac® Library editorial direction: Mark Sachner
World Almanac® Library editors: Monica Rausch and Tea Benduhn
World Almanac® Library art direction: Tammy West
World Almanac® Library designer: Scott Krall
World Almanac® Library production: Jessica Yanke and Robert Kraus

Printed in Canada

1 2 3 4 5 6 7 8 9 10 10 09 08 07 06

In the courtyard of the church in London, they saw a strange sight.

LOOK! A STONE WITH A SWORD IN IT!

Whosoever can draw out this sword is by right the King of England.

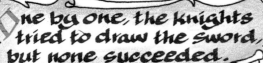

One by one, the knights tried to draw the sword, but none succeeded.

OOF!

AAARGH!

URRGH!

At last, they consulted a famed wizard named Merlin.

THE SWORD WILL NOT BUDGE. WHAT DOES IT MEAN?

THE MAN IS NOT HERE WHO CAN LIFT OUT THE MAGIC SWORD... NOR DO WE KNOW WHERE TO FIND HIM.

Another knight was going to London to attend a tournament. His name was Sir Kay.

ARTHUR, DEAR BROTHER, I'VE FORGOTTEN MY SWORD. WOULD YOU KINDLY RETURN HOME AND FETCH IT?

WITH PLEASURE, KAY.

But on returning home...

THE GATE IS LOCKED, AND NO DOUBT THE WATCHMAN IS SLEEPING. I CAN'T GET IN.

WHAT A SHAME. HOW CAN MY BROTHER ENTER THE TOURNAMENT WITHOUT A SWORD?

HO! THERE'S A SWORD IN THAT COURTYARD, I'LL BORROW IT.

WELL, WELL. THIS IS A BEAUTY!

KAY, LOOK AT THE FINE SWORD I BROUGHT YOU.

WH-WHERE DID YOU G-GET THAT, ARTHUR?

The deadly gift. The King ruled over England for many years, guiding and advising his knights of the Round Table.

REMEMBER, MY FRIENDS, IT IS A KNIGHT'S DUTY TO PROTECT THE WEAK AND FIGHT FOR JUSTICE!

HAIL TO NOBLE KING ARTHUR!

The King's sister, Morgan le Fay, lived in a castle near Camelot. She was an evil woman, jealous of her brother's success.

EVERYONE IS SINGING ARTHUR'S PRAISES -- IT MAKES ME SICK!

HOW CAN I PUT AN END TO MY BROTHER? I MUST THINK OF SOMETHING CLEVER.

HE'S PROTECTED BY MERLIN THE WIZARD. BUT I, TOO, AM A SORCERER. I, TOO, HAVE MAGIC POWERS!

Suddenly... GASP! CHOKE I'M--I'M--

MERCY UPON US! GOOD SIR PATRISE IS DEAD!

THIS FRUIT HAS BEEN POISONED!

Patrise's cousin, Sir Mador, turned on the Queen.

YOU PLOTTED THIS FEAST DELIBERATELY! I ACCUSE YOU OF POISONING MY KINSMAN!

NO. NO... I D-DID NOTHING!

PATRISE HAD NO ENEMIES, SO IT MUST HAVE BEEN YOU. I SAY YOU ALONE ARE TO BLAME!

I SWEAR I'M INNOCENT!

The matter was placed before King Arthur.

MILORD, I DIDN'T DO THIS DEED!

YET IT'S TRUE THAT YOU PLANNED THE BANQUET. THIS IS SERIOUS.

YOUR HIGHNESS, OUR LAW STATES THAT THE QUEEN MUST BE PUT TO DEATH IF MADOR'S ACCUSATION STANDS.

OH NO!

-SOB-

Guinevere pleaded for her life.

I'M INNOCENT, ARTHUR, I KNEW NOTHING OF THE POISONING PLOT.

I'M SORRY, MY DEAR. THIS IS A VERY SERIOUS CHARGE.

ACCORDING TO THE RULES OF CHIVALRY, YOU HAVE ONLY ONE CHANCE. YOU MUST FIND A KNIGHT TO CHAMPION YOU, AND DO BATTLE WITH SIR MADOR.

The knights discussed the matter, but all of them sided with the dead man's cousin.

THE QUEEN ARRANGED THIS FEAST. THE DEATH OF SIR PATRISE WAS HER FAULT.

I WILL NOT DEFEND HER.

NOR I.

NOR I.

Desperate, the Queen turned to an elderly knight who had known her as a child.

PLEASE, SIR BORS, YOU MUST SAVE ME. YOU'RE MY LAST HOPE.

ME? BUT-- VERY WELL. I'LL TRY.

Sir Bors was deeply distressed.

MADOR IS STRONG AND POWERFUL. I CAN NEVER DEFEAT HIM-- B-BUT I'LL DO MY BEST.

KING ARTHUR

MANY PEOPLE HAVE WRITTEN ABOUT KING ARTHUR, BUT NO ONE KNOWS WHO WROTE DOWN THE FIRST STORIES ABOUT HIM. THE STORIES ABOUT KING ARTHUR ARE PART OF THE LEGENDS AND MYTHS OF GREAT BRITAIN'S HISTORY. IN THE PAST, THE TALES WERE PASSED DOWN THROUGH STORIES PEOPLE TOLD ONE ANOTHER. EVENTUALLY PEOPLE BEGAN TO WRITE DOWN THESE STORIES. THE FIRST FORMS OF THESE STORIES APPEARED IN THE WRITTEN POEMS AND HISTORY OF NORTHERN IRELAND AND WALES, A PART OF THE UNITED KINGDOM OF GREAT BRITAIN. THE STORIES BECAME POPULAR WHEN GEOFFREY OF MONMOUTH WROTE ABOUT THEM IN HIS BOOK **HISTORIA REGUM BRITANNIAE** (**HISTORY OF THE KINGS OF BRITAIN**) IN ABOUT 1136. SOME PEOPLE BELIEVE KING ARTHUR WAS A REAL PERSON WHO LIVED LONG AGO. THEY BELIEVE HE MIGHT HAVE BECOME FAMOUS WHEN GERMANIC PEOPLE INVADED GREAT BRITAIN AND ARTHUR LED HIS PEOPLE IN BATTLES AGAINST THE INVADERS. OTHER PEOPLE BELIEVE KING ARTHUR WAS NEVER A REAL PERSON. SOME OF THE STORIES ABOUT ARTHUR ARE ABOUT CAMELOT, A KINGDOM THAT WAS RULED BY ARTHUR AND HIS KNIGHTS OF THE ROUND TABLE. OTHER STORIES ARE ABOUT HIS KNIGHTS, WHO GO ON "QUESTS," OR JOURNEYS TO FIND VALUABLE ITEMS OR KNOWLEDGE OR TO SAVE PEOPLE. IN MANY OF THE QUESTS, THE KNIGHTS ARE LOOKING FOR THE HOLY GRAIL, A DISH OR CUP THAT CHRISTIANS BELIEVE JESUS CHRIST ONCE USED.

HALT, WRETCHED KNAVES! DON QUIXOTE DE LA MANCHA *CHALLENGES* YOU!

WHO'S *THAT*?

IS THIS A *JOKE*?

NO! THE OLD FOOL IS *ATTACKING* US!

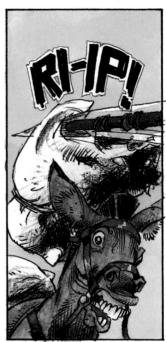

RI-IP!

THE JOLT OF THE LANCE CAUSED QUIXOTE TO LOSE HIS BALANCE.

YOU *IDIOT!* WHY DID YOU RUIN OUR *GOODS*?

TAKE *THAT!*

GIVE HIM *ANOTHER!*

ANGRILY, THE MERCHANTS WENT ON THEIR WAY.

ZOUNDS! MY HELMET IS *WRECKED!* AND SO IS THE *REST* OF ME.

QUIXOTE'S SERVANTS CARRIED HIM HOME.

I *KNEW* THIS WOULD HAPPEN.

POOR MASTER! ≥SOB≤

THEY PUT HIM TO BED AND SENT FOR THE DOCTOR (WHO WAS ALSO THE TOWN BARBER).

LUCKILY, NOTHING'S BROKEN. SEE THAT HE GETS PLENTY OF REST.

YES, SIR.

BUT REST WAS NOT PART OF DON QUIXOTE'S PLAN... AND IN THE MORNING...

I AM READY TO RIDE AGAIN. BUT ALAS, I HAVE NO *HELMET.*

GAD*ZOOKS!* THE BARBER FORGOT HIS SHAVING BASIN. IT'S *JUST* THE THING!

PLACING THE BRASS BOWL ON HIS HEAD, QUIXOTE DRESSED QUICKLY AND SLIPPED OUTSIDE.

TIPTOE, ROZINANTE. TIPTOE!

NOW I MUST FIND A SQUIRE TO SERVE ME. *EVERY* KNIGHT HAS A LOYAL SQUIRE.

IN THE TOWN OF LA MANCHA LIVED A POOR, SIMPLE-MINDED SOUL NAMED SANCHO PANZA.

GOOD SANCHO, I AM GOING TO MAKE YOU RICH AND FAMOUS!

HA, HA! VERY FUNNY. VERY GOOD JOKE, SEÑOR QUIXOTE.

I **TOLD** YOU SO, MASTER! I **TOLD** YOU THEY WERE **WINDMILLS**, NOT **GIANTS!**

GOOD SANCHO, IT IS CLEAR TO ME AN **EVIL SORCERER CHANGED** THE GIANTS TO WINDMILLS AT THE VERY **LAST** MOMENT.

BUT MASTER

HELP ME OVER TO POOR ROZINANTE, THE GIANTS HAVE CAUSED HIM MUCH HARM.

JUST THEN, SOME HORSEMEN WENT BY, TAKING A HERD OF MARES TO THE TOWN FAIR.

ROZINANTE WAS OLD AND FEEBLE, BUT LIKE HIS MASTER, HE HAD A ROMANTIC NATURE.

HE **LEAPED** UP AND TROTTED TOWARD THE MARES.

GAD-**ZOOKS!** WHERE IS HE **GOING**?

BATTERED AND BRUISED, THE TRAVELLERS CREPT INTO A GROVE OF TREES.

COME, LET US REST AND HAVE SOMETHING TO EAT.

ALL WE HAVE, SIRE, IS BREAD AND STALE CHEESE.

BREAD AND STALE CHEESE! A TRUE BANQUET!

NOW THAT I'M WORKING FOR A FAMOUS KNIGHT, I THOUGHT THE FOOD WOULD BE BETTER.

WE DO NOT NEED FOOD FOR THE BODY, SANCHO. WE NEED FOOD FOR THE SOUL.

WELL, ALL THIS ACTIVITY IS MAKING ME SLEEPY. YAWN-N-

YES--SLEEP, GOOD SQUIRE. I WILL SIT HERE AND COMPOSE A POEM TO MY LADY DULCINEA.

A TORTURED MAN, I WEEP AND WAIL, MY SUFFERING'S TO NO AVAIL, FAR AWAY, SHE IS NOT NEAR... I MISS MY DULCINEA DEAR!

MIGUEL DE CERVANTES

MIGUEL DE CERVANTES SAAVEDRA WAS A SPANISH AUTHOR AND PLAYWRIGHT WHOSE NOVEL **DON QUIXOTE DE LA MANCHA** IS OFTEN SEEN AS ONE OF THE FIRST MODERN NOVELS. CERVANTES WAS BORN IN 1547 IN A SMALL TOWN NEAR MADRID, SPAIN. HIS FATHER WAS AN APOTHECARY, OR PHARMACIST, AND A SURGEON. WHILE GROWING UP, CERVANTES MOVED FROM PLACE TO PLACE WITH HIS FAMILY WHILE HIS FATHER FOUND WORK. CERVANTES EVENTUALLY STUDIED IN MADRID AND ROME BEFORE BECOMING A SOLDIER IN 1570. HE FOUGHT IN SEVERAL BATTLES, PERMANENTLY INJURING HIS LEFT HAND IN ONE OF THEM. ON HIS RETURN HOME TO SPAIN, IN 1575, HIS SHIP WAS CAPTURED BY THE TURKS, AND HE WAS TAKEN PRISONER. THE TURKS HELD HIM FOR A LARGE RANSOM, WHICH HIS FAMILY COULD NOT AFFORD. HE TRIED TO ESCAPE SEVERAL TIMES, AND HE WAS FINALLY RELEASED IN 1580. CERVANTES THEN BEGAN WRITING, FIRST PLAYS AND THEN NOVELS. HE WROTE HIS FIRST NOVEL, **LA GALATEA**, IN 1585, BUT IT DID NOT GET MUCH NOTICE FROM THE PUBLIC. THE FIRST PART OF **DON QUIXOTE DE LA MANCHA**, PUBLISHED IN 1605, HOWEVER, WAS A SUCCESS. MANY AUTHORS AT THE TIME TRIED TO IMITATE HIM AND PUBLISHED THEIR OWN "PART TWO" TO THE STORY, UNTIL CERVANTES FINALLY PUBLISHED HIS PART TWO IN 1615. CERVANTES WAS ALSO WRITING OTHER NOVELS AND PLAYS AT THAT TIME. BETWEEN 1613 AND 1615, HE PUBLISHED A COLLECTION OF SHORT NOVELS AND TWO COLLECTIONS OF PLAYS. CERVANTES MARRIED CATALINA DE SALAZAR Y PALACIOS, WHO WAS EIGHTEEN YEARS YOUNGER THAN HIM, IN 1584. HE DIED IN 1616, THE SAME YEAR WILLIAM SHAKESPEARE PASSED AWAY. HIS IMAGE HAS SINCE BEEN PLACED ON SPANISH POSTAGE STAMPS AND ON EUROPEAN COINS.

AT THE TURN OF THE CENTURY IN LONDON, ENGLAND...

ONE DAY DURING THE HOLIDAY SEASON, I PAID A CALL ON MY OLD FRIEND SHERLOCK HOLMES.

AS USUAL, I FOUND SHERLOCK HARD AT WORK IN HIS BAKER STREET LODGINGS.

AH, THERE, WATSON. COME IN, COME IN!

I'M NOT DISTURBING YOU?

NOT AT ALL. I'M JUST STUDYING THIS INTERESTING HAT.

WHAT'S SO INTERESTING ABOUT AN OLD DERBY?

WELL, I KNOW THAT THE OWNER'S NAME IS HARRY BROWN. HE'S ELDERLY AND POOR AND CAN'T AFFORD GAS LIGHT AT HOME. HE'S INTELLIGENT, BUT DOWN ON HIS LUCK.

HOW DID YOU LEARN ALL THAT?

SIMPLE, WATSON. WITH THIS MAGNIFYING GLASS I CAN READ HIS NAME FAINTLY. I ALSO FOUND GRAY HAIRS IN THE LINING.

HARRY BROWN

SEE THESE WAX STAINS? BROWN CARRIES A CANDLE AT HOME. NOTE HOW THE BAND IS TORN?

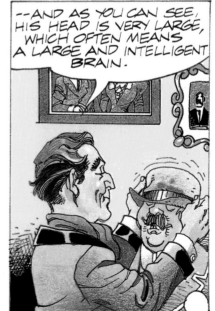

--AND AS YOU CAN SEE, HIS HEAD IS VERY LARGE, WHICH OFTEN MEANS A LARGE AND INTELLIGENT BRAIN.

YOU ASTOUND ME, HOLMES. WHERE DID THE HAT COME FROM?

AN UNUSUAL STORY, WATSON--

IT SEEMS THAT OUR ELDERLY FRIEND, BROWN, WAS HEADING HOME A FEW NIGHTS AGO CARRYING A HOLIDAY GOOSE...

"A COUPLE OF TOUGHS SAW HIM AND DECIDED TO TAKE THE GOOSE..."

LET'S GRAB IT, ALF.

"IN THE SCRAMBLE, BROWN FOUGHT BACK..."

STOP!

HELP!

"SWINGING HIS CANE, HE SMASHED A SHOP WINDOW."

KRAK!

"AT THAT MOMENT, CONSTABLE PETERS CAME AROUND THE CORNER, SAW THE FIGHT, AND RUSHED FORWARD."

"WHEN THE TOUGHS SAW HIM, THEY TURNED AND RAN. OLD BROWN WAS CONFUSED. HE THOUGHT HE'D BE ARRESTED FOR BREAKING THE WINDOW, SO HE RAN, TOO. ...LEAVING HAT AND GOOSE BEHIND."

"PETERS BROUGHT THE ITEMS TO ME."

YOU WERE NEARBY, SIR. I DIDN'T KNOW WHAT *ELSE* TO DO.

QUITE RIGHT, PETERS. THE GOOSE IS LIABLE TO SPOIL. YOU MAY AS WELL TAKE IT HOME FOR DINNER.

...AND THAT, WATSON, IS HOW I WOUND UP WITH MR. BROWN'S DERBY.

POOR OLD FOOL. I'M SURE HE MISSES IT.

JUST THEN-- CONSTABLE PETERS TO SEE YOU, SIR.

SHOW HIM IN, MRS. HUDSON.

AH, THERE, PETERS. HOW WAS THE HOLIDAY GOOSE?

DELICIOUS, SIR. BUT WHEN MY WIFE CUT IT OPEN TO PREPARE IT--

--LOOK WHAT SHE FOUND *INSIDE!*

BY GEORGE! THE FAMOUS MORCAR *BLUE DIAMOND!*

IT WAS FOUND YEARS AGO IN SOUTHERN CHINA AND IS NOW OWNED BY THE COUNTESS OF MORCAR. THROUGH THE YEARS, MEN HAVE CLIMBED HIGH MOUNTAINS, BRAVED RAGING RIVERS, AND CROSSED BURNING DESERTS TO WIN THIS PRICELESS JEWEL!

WASN'T IT STOLEN RECENTLY FROM THE COUNTESS?

YES. I HAVE THE NEWS REPORT HERE.

⸮AHEM⸮ ON THE TWENTY-SECOND OF DECEMBER, THE WORLD-FAMOUS BLUE DIAMOND OF COUNTESS MORCAR WAS TAKEN FROM HER SUITE AT THE HOTEL COSMOPOLITAN. A PLUMBER NAMED HORNER HAS BEEN ARRESTED, BUT HE DENIES THE CHARGES.

THE COUNTESS HAS OFFERED A REWARD OF 1,000 POUNDS* FOR THE JEWEL'S RETURN.

* IN THOSE DAYS, 1 POUND EQUALED $5.

REPORT THIS TO SCOTLAND YARD, PETERS. TELL THEM I'M KEEPING THE DIAMOND SAFELY LOCKED UP.

YES, SIR.

AN *ODD* BUSINESS, HOLMES. DO YOU THINK THE PLUMBER IS GUILTY?

HMM--THE SECRET TO OUR MYSTERY, WATSON, RESTS WITH THE OWNER OF THIS OLD HAT.

HOW CAN WE *FIND* HIM? THERE ARE *THOUSANDS* OF HARRY BROWNS IN LONDON.

WE'LL TRY ADVERTISING.

LET'S SEE--

FOUND: ON THE CORNER OF GOODGE STREET, A GOOSE AND A FELT DERBY HAT. OWNER CAN HAVE THESE BY APPLYING AT 6:30 THIS EVENING TO 221-B BAKER STREET.

HOLMES SENT FOR A GROUP OF STREET BOYS. HE CALLED THEM THE "BAKER STREET IRREGULARS," AND THEY OFTEN HELPED IN HIS WORK.

WIGGINS, I WANT YOU AND YOUR LADS TO RUSH THESE TO ALL THE PAPERS-- THE GLOBE, THE STAR, THE EVENING NEWS, THE ECHO--*ALL* OF THEM.

YES, SIR, MR. HOLMES.

GET THESE ADS PLACED IN TIME, AND THERE'S A SHILLING FOR EACH OF YOU.

DO YOU THINK THEY'LL MAKE IT, HOLMES?

OH, YES! I CAN ALWAYS COUNT ON THE BAKER STREET IRREGULARS.

"FULL OF CURIOSITY, I RETURNED TO BAKER STREET THAT EVENING AT 6:30. A FEW MINUTES LATER."

ANOTHER VISITOR.

I CAME IN ANSWER TO YOUR AD, SIR.

YOUR NAME, MY GOOD MAN?

HARRY BROWN.

GOOD! I AM HAPPY TO RETURN YOUR HAT.

THANK YOU, SIR! THANK YOU INDEED.

UNFORTUNATELY, THE GOOSE WAS STARTING TO GO BAD, SO WE HAD TO EAT IT.

OF COURSE. I UNDERSTAND. IT COULDN'T BE HELPED.

--HMM--

WE--ER--SAVED THE "INNARDS" FOR YOU. THE NECK, GIZZARD AND SO ON. WOULD YOU LIKE THOSE?

HEAVENS, NO. BUT THANK YOU ANYWAY.

IN THAT CASE, YOU DESERVE A FRESH GOOSE: PLEASE ACCEPT THIS WITH MY COMPLIMENTS.

OH, THANK YOU, SIR! MRS. BROWN WILL BE MOST PLEASED.

BY THE WAY, BROWN, WHERE DID THE *FIRST* GOOSE COME FROM?

THE ALPHA INN ON HUNT STREET. THE OWNER GAVE THEM AS HOLIDAY GIFTS TO ALL HIS FRIENDS.

CLEARLY, WATSON, HE KNOWS NOTHING ABOUT THE DIAMOND. OUR NEXT STOP IS THE ALPHA INN.

BUT KINDLY EXCUSE ME FOR A MOMENT.

"I PACED BACK AND FORTH, WAITING IMPATIENTLY TO FIND OUT WHAT HOLMES WAS UP TO. THEN--"

♪ COME ALONG. WE'VE NO TIME TO WASTE. ♪

I B-BEG YOUR PARDON, MADAM?

FOR HEAVEN'S SAKE, WATSON-- IT'S *ME*. I'M WELL KNOWN AT THE ALPHA, AND I WANT TO KEEP THIS INVESTIGATION SECRET.

HOLMES, YOU NEVER CEASE TO AMAZE ME! I WOULD NEVER HAVE GUESSED WHO YOU WERE!

WHY, YOU-- YOU CAN EVEN CHANGE THE QUALITY OF YOUR *VOICE!*

ALL PART OF THE JOB, MY DEAR WATSON.

AFTER DINNER AT THE ALPHA INN, HOLMES SENT FOR THE OWNER.

THAT WAS AN EXCELLENT GOOSE DINNER, MY GOOD MAN.

WHY, THANK YOU KINDLY, MA'AM.

JUST THEN--

PSST! LISTEN, I MUST TALK TO YOU ABOUT MY GOOSE--

YOU AGAIN?

ONE OF THOSE YOU GAVE AWAY BELONGED TO ME, AND I WANT--

I'M SICK AND TIRED OF YOU PESTERING ME EVERY DAY!

HELP!

GET OUT! LEAVE ME ALONE! YOU AND YOUR BLOOMIN' GEESE!

ALPHA INN

QUICK, WATSON! WE MUST FOLLOW THAT MAN!

I THINK HE HAS THE ANSWERS WE NEED!

I'M SICK OF THAT LITTLE PEST!

-PUFF- -PUFF-

I OBJECT TO THIS OUTRAGE! WHO, MADAM, ARE *YOU*?

MY NAME IS SHERLOCK HOLMES.

H-HOLMES? THE GREAT DETECTIVE?

PRECISELY-- AND *YOUR* NAME, SIR?

R-ROBINSON. JOHN ROBINSON.

THAT IS A *LIE*. YOU ARE JAMES RYDER, CLERK AT THE HOTEL COSMOPOLITAN. I RECOGNIZED YOU EASILY.

CONFUSED, RYDER AGREED TO ACCOMPANY US TO HOLMES' LODGINGS. HE SEEMED VERY FRIGHTENED.

NOW THEN, WHAT'S ALL THIS ABOUT A MISSING GOOSE?

HE TRIED TO BLUFF.

I D-DON'T KNOW WHAT YOU MEAN, MR. HOLMES.

I'M TALKING ABOUT A CERTAIN *GOOSE* THAT LAID A VERY VALUABLE EGG.

IS *THIS* THE EGG, MR. RYDER?

THE BLUE DIAMOND!

I FEAR OUR FRIEND HAS FAINTED, DR. WATSON.

NO PROBLEM, HOLMES. I'LL BRING HIM AROUND.

RYDER RECOVERED IN A FEW MINUTES...

NOW THEN. LET US HAVE THE TRUTH.

V-VERY WELL, SIR. I'LL TELL ALL...

MY PARTNER IN ALL THIS WAS MISS CUSAK, PERSONAL MAID TO THE COUNTESS.

SHE TOLD ME ABOUT THE PRECIOUS DIAMOND, AND WE AGREED TO SEIZE IT.

"I WAITED UNTIL THE PLUMBER, JOHN HORNER, WAS WORKING ALONE IN THE SUITE."

"IT WAS AN EASY MATTER TO PRY OPEN HER JEWEL CASE AND REMOVE THE BOX WITH THE DIAMOND..."

"...THEN MISS CUSAK GAVE THE ALARM."

HELP! THIEVES! POLICE!

"WHEN THE POLICE CAME, I ACCUSED THE PLUMBER, WHO ALREADY HAD A POLICE RECORD."

I **SAW** HIM TAKE IT FROM THE COUNTESS' ROOM.

NO, NO!

COME ALONG!

HMM...AND WHAT ABOUT THE BLUE DIAMOND?

I HAD IT IN MY POCKET, BUT I WAS TERRIFIED.

I EXPECTED THE POLICE TO SEARCH ME AND SEARCH MY ROOM. I WAS IN A PANIC, CRAZY WITH FEAR, THEN I HAD AN IDEA...

DRIVER, TAKE ME TO THE OAKSHOTT FARM, ON BRIXTON ROAD.

'OP IN, SIR.

"MY SISTER, EMMA, HAS A GOOSE FARM IN BRIXTON. SHE HAD PROMISED ME A CHRISTMAS GOOSE-- WHICH MADE ME THINK OF A PERFECT HIDING PLACE!"

"QUICKLY, I SEIZED A LARGE GOOSE WITH A BLACK TAIL AND SHOVED THE JEWEL DOWN ITS THROAT."

"THEN I WENT INTO THE HOUSE."

GOOD DAY, EMMA. I'VE COME FOR MY GOOSE.

FINE, JAMES. FIRST SIT AND HAVE A CUP OF TEA.

HOME SWEET HOME

"I FELT SAFE AT LAST. AFTER THE TEA, I TOOK MY GOOSE AND LEFT."

ENJOY IT, JAMES.

I WILL INDEED.

WHAT HAPPENED THEN?

BACK IN LONDON, I CARRIED THE GOOSE TO A MAN I KNEW WHO BOUGHT STOLEN GOODS...

..."BUT WHEN WE CUT THE GOOSE OPEN--"

WAIT, NOW! THERE'S NO DIAMOND HERE!

WHAT?!

"REALIZING THAT I'D TAKEN THE WRONG GOOSE, I RACED BACK TO THE FARM."

FASTER, DRIVER, FASTER!

EMMA, WHERE ARE THE GEESE? I MADE A MISTAKE!

WHY-- THEY'RE ALL GONE, JAMES!

GONE?!

I SHIPPED THEM ALL TO THE OWNER OF THE ALPHA INN ON HUNT STREET.

"I RUSHED BACK TO LONDON, BUT IT WAS A LONG TRIP."

ALPHA INN.

INNKEEPER, THOSE GEESE YOU BOUGHT... ONE OF THEM IS MINE!

THEY'RE NOT HERE, MY FRIEND.

N-NOT HERE?

I GAVE THAT LOT AWAY AS HOLIDAY GIFTS. THE LAST WENT AN HOUR AGO.

OH, NO! YOU CAN'T! I MEAN, ONE OF THEM BELONGED TO ME, AND--

STOP BOTHERING ME! I HAVE WORK TO DO.

I WENT BACK AGAIN AND AGAIN, AND THAT'S WHEN YOU CAUGHT ME. HAVE MERCY, MR. HOLMES.

YOU DESERVE *NO* MERCY, BUT AT LEAST YOU HAVE BEEN HONEST, WHICH WILL HELP YOUR CASE.

"WE SENT FOR CONSTABLE PETERS AND HAD RYDER ARRESTED."

COME ALONG, NOW.

DON'T FORGET TO PICK UP HIS ACCOMPLICE, MISS CUSAK.

AND NOW, WATSON, SHALL WE STEP ROUND TO THE HOTEL COSMOPOLITAN AND RETURN THIS LITTLE BAUBLE TO THE COUNTESS?

A CAPITAL IDEA, HOLMES.

"ON THE WAY, I MENTIONED THE REWARD!"

A THOUSAND POUNDS IS A LOT OF MONEY.

I AGREE.

"PERHAPS IT COULD BE USED TO ESTABLISH A SCHOLARSHIP FUND FOR MY BAKER STREET IRREGULARS."

WONDERFUL! MAYBE SOMEDAY ONE OF THOSE RASCALS WILL TURN OUT TO BE A DETECTIVE LIKE THE BRILLIANT *SHERLOCK HOLMES!*

MY DEAR WATSON, YOU ARE TOO KIND!

THE END

SIR ARTHUR CONAN DOYLE

SIR ARTHUR CONAN DOYLE WAS BORN ON MAY 22, 1959, TO IRISH PARENTS IN EDINBURGH, SCOTLAND. HIS MOTHER WAS A GREAT STORYTELLER, AND HE GREW UP LISTENING TO HER TALES. WHILE IN SCHOOL, DOYLE FASCINATED FRIENDS WITH HIS OWN STORIES. HE LATER WENT TO MEDICAL SCHOOL AND BECAME A DOCTOR. IN BETWEEN PATIENT VISITS, DOYLE BEGAN WRITING. HE PUBLISHED A FEW SHORT STORIES BEFORE WRITING THE NOVEL **A STUDY IN SCARLET**, IN 1887, IN WHICH HE INTRODUCED THE CHARACTER SHERLOCK HOLMES. THE CHARACTER, WITH HIS LOGIC AND DEDUCTIVE REASONING, WAS SAID TO BE BASED ON A TEACHER DOYLE HAD HAD IN MEDICAL SCHOOL. HOLMES BECAME AN INSTANT FAVORITE AMONG READERS, BUT DESPITE HIS POPULARITY, DOYLE GREW TIRED OF WRITING ABOUT HIM. IN 1893, DOYLE HAD HIM DIE IN THE STORY "THE FINAL PROBLEM." READERS, HOWEVER, WERE UPSET BY THE DEATH. DOYLE THEN WROTE **THE HOUNDS OF BASKERVILLES**, IN 1902, AS A TALE THAT OCCURRED BEFORE HOLMES'S DEATH. IN 1903, HE WROTE "THE EMPTY HOUSE," IN WHICH HOLMES REAPPEARED. THE STORY EXPLAINED THAT HOLMES HAD FAKED HIS DEATH TO AVOID HIS ENEMIES. DOYLE WOULD WRITE A TOTAL OF FIFTY-SIX SHORT STORIES AND FOUR NOVELS FEATURING HOLMES AND HIS COMPANION, DR. WATSON. DOYLE HAD TWO CHILDREN WITH HIS FIRST WIFE, LOUISA HAWKINS, BEFORE HER DEATH IN 1906. IN 1907, HE MARRIED JEAN LECKIE, AND THEY HAD THREE CHILDREN TOGETHER. HE WAS KNIGHTED BY GREAT BRITAIN'S KING EDWARD II FOR HIS WORK AS A DOCTOR DURING THE SOUTH AFRICAN BOER WAR. DOYLE LOST HIS ELDEST SON DURING WORLD WAR I. IN HIS LATER YEARS, DOYLE BECAME INTERESTED IN THE PARANORMAL. HE DIED ON JULY 7, 1930, OF A HEART ATTACK.